Proposal Development Secrets
Win More, Work Smarter, and Get Home On Time

By Matt Handal

Dedication

This book is dedicated to my loving wife, Molly, and my son Logan. Thank you for forgiving the time I was away developing proposals and could not be with you.

Table of Contents

Why Do I Want To Read A Book About Proposal Development? Yuck!

WHO IS THIS BOOK FOR?

This book was written for who I was a few years ago, a proposal/marketing coordinator or manager at a small to medium-sized professional services firm (i.e. those who provide services like architecture, engineering, construction, IT consulting, legal, accounting, and so forth).

This book is for you. You don't have a huge team of people helping you put proposals together. More likely, it's you and a few "professionals" producing the entire proposal.

People simply don't recognize the stress you are under. If the proposal doesn't get to the client, you get the blame. You are the one responsible for making sure everybody does their piece, does it well, and does it on time. Not to mention, you have to put the thing together and get it out the door. One tiny screw up could mean thousands or even millions of dollars of lost revenue for your firm.

There are many things that can go wrong during the development of a proposal. You don't want to experience any of them, but you've probably experienced more than your share. You've seen late nights and maybe even a few holidays in the office.

This book is not going to give you some convoluted 100-step process for developing proposals. We won't discuss blue teams and red teams because you don't have teams of people working on your proposals. It's not going to tell you whether to use Adobe Indesign, Microsoft Word, or Powerpoint. It won't go into whether to staple or bind your proposal or which font to use.

It is going to focus on the cold hard realities of the proposal business and provide you with some strategies to help you get home to the people and things that you love.

THE PROPOSAL MANAGER

For the sake of this book, I'm going to refer to you as the proposal manager. You might not have the words "manager" or "proposal" in your official title. But in reality, that's what you are doing, managing the development of the proposal.

WHAT ABOUT VPS AND PRESIDENTS?

I'm not saying that this book won't help you if you're an officer of a firm or even if you are starting your own small business. Sure, some of the topics and advice in this book will be very helpful to you. But don't expect to relate to everything I say, because it's coming from the prospective of the proposal manager. The proposal manager can't snap his or her fingers and make people do their bidding. They have to employ tactics that will help make sure everybody does what they need to do and a winning proposal is delivered to the client, on time.

The proposal manager has to "own" the entire process while being smart, vigilant, creative, and understanding.

WHY SHOULD YOU LISTEN TO ME?

Let me start by saying that I'm probably not the world's foremost expert on proposal development. However, over the last decade, I've had the luxury of delivering thousands of proposals to corporate and government clients in every state and overseas. I've proposed on and won professional consulting assignments ranging in value from a few thousand to many millions of dollars. I've produced letter proposals and proposals that were submitted in multiple three-ring binders.

Unlike many proposal managers I have spoken to, I've also written technical and pricing sections of proposals. I've single-handedly written and produced entire proposals for large contracts, and won. A few of those proposals were long shots, at best.

I've also made mistakes. I've been kicked out of procurements (once). I've had proposals not delivered on time (and had them ultimately accepted — we'll get into how to do that). I was also shocked to learn that the absolute worst proposal I ever submitted actually won (I'll tell you about that one too).

I've evaluated the proposals of others when they were proposing to me. I've also spoken in great detail to ex-procurement officials about the sometimes questionable tactics they use when evaluating proposals (which I'll let you in on).

If you are looking for real insights into the proposal business, if you want to work smarter and not harder, and if you care deeply about the outcome of the proposals you produce, this is the book for you.

How To Use This Book

Read This If You're Not Quite Ready To Get To The Advice

This isn't a "how-to" book. I'm not going to take you step by step through the process of developing a proposal. I'm not going to discuss how to identify prospective clients or find requests for proposals. There are hundreds of other books that will show you how to do those things. That's not what this book is about.

Instead, this book is made up of a series of "how-to-do-betters." Sure, you can read the book cover to cover (or whatever the Kindle equivalent is). But you can also pick and choose chapters to read based on where you feel you need improvement or what topics interest you.

I'm assuming you've participated in the development of a proposal or two. If not, this probably isn't the book you want to start out with.

However you decide to read this book, I think you'll find valuable insights that might just make proposal development a little less taxing and a lot more rewarding.

Chapter 1:

Corporate Vs. Government Clients: Is There A Difference?

And Should You Get Hung Up On It?

There are differences associated with the proposal processes of corporate and government clients, but the main difference has to do with obligation.

While corporate clients may have internal procedures they stick to, they have very little, if any, obligation when it comes to how they evaluate proposals. They can reject your proposal or choose whoever they want for any reason. This is why you don't see many bid protests in the corporate sector.

Government clients have obligations, which vary depending on their governing body. Those obligations are a double-edged sword for you. If you fail to completely fill out a form, or you use a font or margin they did not specify, you stand a good chance of your proposal being disqualified. This is because they may be obligated to disqualify you.

Government agencies can be obligated to select winning proposals based entirely on price. They could also be restricted from using price as the deciding factor. They may also be obligated to make their selection decisions public, but that's not always the case.

They may be obligated to choose a firm that incorporates participation from what are referred to as socially disadvantaged businesses (which could include minority or veteran-owned businesses).

The bottom line is: don't get hung up on whether you are proposing to a government or corporate client. While there are differences, my advice will be consistent. Always develop your proposal in strict compliance with the client's request for proposal or qualifications (which we'll refer to as the RFP).

Chapter 2:

Proposal Myths - Debunked

Don't Believe Everything You Hear

Before we get into "how the sausage is made," I want to cover a few important topics that you have to understand before creating the best proposals.

The first topic is what I refer to as the proposal myths. These are things you hear executives or sales people say that, while somewhat rooted in reality, fail to tell the whole story. Let's explore a few of these proposal myths.

IS IT REALLY ALL ABOUT RELATIONSHIPS?

There is a sermon that far too many people in the proposal business preach. I hear it all the time from experienced "marketing experts." Over and over again they say, "Don't submit a proposal unless you have a relationship." They'll also say, "Don't waste your time and money subscribing to lead services, you won't get anywhere without relationships."

If you consider the various types of firms providing professional services, this is not good advice. What these people are saying does not apply to all businesses.

Say for example, you are a construction contractor who does "low-bid" work, in which the lowest responsible bidder is awarded the work. That's a case where it might be foolish not to respond because you don't have a relationship, especially if you can beat the competitors on price.

Here's another example. Let's say you are a building design firm that designs BSL-4 laboratories (labs where they work on highly contagious bugs). There are not many firms that have extensive experience designing those. While the owner might prefer choosing someone they have a "relationship" with, my sense is that they would much rather keep that Ebola virus from escaping and killing us all. So in that case, qualifications matter.

Now I love my drinking buddies, but I wouldn't hire them to design my nuclear power plant. If I was suspected of murder, I wouldn't hire my friend, the corporate litigator, to defend me. I think you get the drift.

"Relationships" Don't Win You Work

"Relationships" are certainly a factor in the decision making process. But unfortunately, you are not getting the whole story about relationships. It's not really a relationship, per say, that influences decisions. You have to break the concept of relationships down to the molecular level and gain a better understanding of what exactly is it about relationships that influence decisions.

For example, it is true that, "Studies show that people hire those they like." But these studies talk about the scientific term "liking." Liking is why Kelly Ripa, the daytime talk show host, is the spokesperson for my bank and my hospital. Science shows that because I think Kelly Ripa is a swell gal, I am more likely to give those businesses with her mug on their ads my cash and/or blood. My personal feelings toward Kelly are transferred to their product, even though I have never met her and could not claim any type of relationship.

Liking is the reason one of my teachers very inappropriately told the dumb girl in my high school to "wear something slutty" to her college entrance interview. She did and she got in because of the "liking effect" and its ability to influence decisions.

Liking is also used by researchers to determine the addictiveness of drugs. Liking is something that has been studied extensively and there is a lot more to it than you might realize.

The Math is Wrong

People also cite firms who only submitted on opportunities where they had an ongoing relationship and increased their proposal win percentage. The problem with this thinking is proposal win percentage, by itself, is not necessarily a great measurement tool. Your goal is probably revenue, not proposal wins. If you win 50% of $100,000 is it better than 30% of $250,000? I'd rather take the 30%.

IF WE PROPOSE AND LOSE, AT LEAST WE GOT OUR NAME OUT THERE

If only I had a dime for every time I heard this pile of nonsense. It really depends on the quality of your proposal. If your proposal is the second best, I would agree you "got your name out there." At my current firm, we were awarded a large public contract after losing the proposal competition. I guess the client reconsidered after working a bit with our competition.

On the other hand, consider this. The initial elimination process is often quick and decisive. In addition, it may be done by an assistant rather than a decision maker. It is very likely that a poor proposal will never make it into the hands of the decision makers. So, to propose on something you are not qualified for, or can't sell, can be a monumental waste of your time.

WE HAVE AN INSIDE CONNECTION, OUR PROPOSAL DOESN'T MATTER

Let's talk about the worst proposal ever submitted. Of course, it was submitted by me many years ago to a corporate client. Let me give you an example of how bad this proposal was. Not only did we spell the client's name (company name) wrong, the technical approach we submitted was way off. To make matters worse, we had never worked for this client before.

To my utter shock, we won. This was a proposal for a couple hundred thousand dollars, so it wasn't insignificant. I just couldn't believe they even accepted that proposal.

Months later, I was complaining to my boss. I asked, "If my work product doesn't influence the client's decision, what's the point of my job?"

My boss just laughed and said, "That guy owed me a favor."

That's a clear example of how a firm can have an inside track on a proposal competition. However, consider this: what if someone else's boss had done that guy an even bigger favor? You never really know what is going on behind the scenes. So, to submit a proposal that is anything less than outstanding is setting yourself up for disaster.

I was naive to think the proposal's quality always weighed heavily with the decision maker. That's not the world we live in. But it is also naive to think that a proposal's quality doesn't weigh into the selection.

As an experienced proposal manager once said to me, "A great proposal can't always win you the job, but a terrible proposal can always lose you the job."

WE HAVE A _____% CHANCE OF WINNING THIS JOB

I know people who swear they can predict, with reasonable certainty, their firm's work backlog based on proposal submissions. They say, "We win 10% of the proposals we're identified as a subconsultant on. Multiply the value of all our proposals by 10% to get the volume of work we can anticipate."

If the value of your proposals and win percentage doesn't deviate that much, I can see the reasonableness of this approach. However, someone's prediction of win probability should have no bearing on the quality of your work.

Let me play the devil's advocate here. Let's say you propose, as a prime, on a $100,000 assignment. You learn that two other firms submitted. At face value, the likelihood of winning the job is roughly 33%. But proposals are not like rolling dice or flipping a coin. There are many more variables, like price, quality of proposal, relationships, and even the client's previous experience with the firms submitting. If you knew the variables, you could do a monte carlo simulation to determine the probability. But you simply don't know all the variables.

Therefore, I submit to you that it is impossible to predict, with any certainty, your probability of winning an individual proposal competition unless you have credible inside information. I think the real question is, "Based on everything we know, do we have a reasonable shot?"

This is where a quality "go/no procedure" comes into play. There has been a great deal written about creating a go/no go process. An internet search should bring up several helpful examples for your specific industry. I strongly agree that you can't go after everything and I do believe in the power of a good go/no go process.

If you can truly predict the likelihood of proposal wins, you're in the wrong business: Vegas is calling.

The bottom line is since nobody can accurately predict proposal wins, you shouldn't change the approach to your work just because someone throws some erroneous prediction your way.

IT'S ALL ABOUT COST

Sometimes it is all about cost. But with professional services, that's usually not the case. Clients hire those who provide professional services because they need help with something outside their area of expertise. Typically, they have a budget to procure these services.

When you think about it, we rarely base any buying decision entirely on price, let alone those that have significant consequences.

Would you base your decision to hire an attorney to defend you against murder allegations entirely on price? That would be insane. Do you walk into a car dealership and say, "I want the cheapest car on the lot?" Not if you want to survive the drive home. When you chose your heart surgeon, did you base that decision entirely on price? Not if you are alive to read this book!

It is reasonable to select the lowest cost option that satisfies your needs. But if all the choices are within your budget, price usually becomes a non-factor. If you can afford it, and it makes sense, you go with the best.

Before listening to anything people say about proposals, think about how you make buying decisions. Clients are people, just like you.

Chapter 3:

You As The Proposal's Advocate

Putting Everything Into Context

As the proposal manager, you are responsible for the proposal. You can't think of yourself as someone who is throwing some information into a template. That's monkey work. You do knowledge work, which means that your knowledge adds value to the overall work product.

As the proposal manager, you must take "ownership" of the proposal. This means you take it upon yourself to control its quality, make sure that everything is consistent, that the proposal adheres to the requirements of the RFP, and you put your firm's "best foot forward" by developing the most persuasive proposal possible.

Whatever needs to be done to make the proposal great, make sure it gets done.

If someone is making changes to the proposal, which you think will reduce its effectiveness, you need to speak up. If you think the wrong people are working on the proposal, speak up. If you think the technical approach is flawed, speak up. If you think there is anything that can be done to make the proposal better, speak up. The proposal cannot speak on its own behalf, so you need to be its advocate. You need to look out for it and be its voice.

Chapter 4:

Proposal Evaluation Practices Clients Don't Want You To Know

Please, Don't Let Them Know I Told You

It is critical to understand how the proposals you submit are being evaluated. Sometimes they are reviewed by a committee who each give an independent and fair assessment on the merits of each proposal. Once the scores are tabulated, an angel comes down and kisses the winning proposal. Then a children's' choir sings.

Other clients take shortcuts because they need to make good decisions quickly and get back to their real job. Let's discuss some of the tactics former procurement officials and buyers have told me they have used.

THE BOX CHECKER

Sometimes there is an evaluation before your proposal gets to the real selection committee. The purpose of this evaluation is to eliminate proposals that didn't follow directions (known as unresponsive) or slim down the pack by eliminating the proposals in which the people or experience doesn't meet some minimum criteria.

This is exactly what the U.S. General Services Administration does before evaluating proposals submitted for their multiple award schedule program, known as the GSA Schedule.

Always assume there will be a box checker. Make sure your proposal strictly follows the requirements set forth in the RFP and that the information provided in your proposal clearly meets the minimum criteria.

It would be a good idea to have your own "box checker" to review the proposal before it goes out.

THE "THREE CARD MONTE"

"The Three Card Monte" isn't something business people talk openly about. In fact, you might not even be aware of it unless you experienced it for yourself!

However, you can be certain that every experienced marketer has either been a victim or profiteer of this scam. Over the years, we have learned to accept the Three Card Monte as a natural part of the business practice. If you quietly sneak up on a group of old wrinkly proposal managers, you may even catch them snickering about it in the dark corners of industry get togethers.

Here is how the Three Card Monte works. You get a call or RFP from a corporate or government client. Typically, it's a client that you have worked with in the past. It's a great opportunity. Maybe the one you've been pre-selling or maybe something that's a little bit of a stretch...but fits within your "go" criteria. The good news is there are only two other firms that have been asked to bid.

You sharpen your pencils and, with your sweat equity, you put together a proposal that would make the angels cry.

You find out, usually pretty quickly, that your firm was not selected. Rather, another firm has swooped in and claimed the prize. Something just doesn't feel right in your gut. You've just fallen victim to one of the oldest procurement tricks in the book.

What Was Going On Behind The Scenes?

Here is what you didn't see. The client had already decided who they were going to pick before the RFP came out. Their procurement agent may have contacted the winning firm and asked them to develop some RFP language for this project (hey, it saves them a heck of a lot of time). The procurement agent may have also asked for the names of two firms that provide these services, but would not match up well to the winning firm's experience or price.

The client's policy probably considers a competitive selection process among three firms to constitute a fair procurement. Three is usually the magic number. But in reality, it is very rare that only three firms are qualified to do the assignment. Three is typically the minimum number of proposers needed, both in the corporate and government sectors.

The client then goes to the two other firms, let's call them marks, to provide them with an RFP and an invitation to bid.

To those new to the proposal world this may seem a little far fetched. But retired procurement people have admitted to me that this is common practice.

Why Do Clients Do This?

Clients have a reason for doing this. Large private clients usually have a rotating group of pre-qualified firms which they give work to (referred to later as the Round Robin). They know if they don't give you any work, you will stop knocking on their door. Often, they try to spread out the work to keep the consultants interested. The Three Card Monte is a vehicle for them to do this. They can also use it as a way to price check the winner.

On the public side, procurement can be a long and drawn-out process. I've waited as long as two years for a government client to go through the process of making a decision. The Three Card Monte is a vehicle for public agency buyers to take a shortcut through the process.

How Do You Recognize The Three Card Monte?

The best way to recognize it is when you are asked to provide RFP language for a client. This doesn't always mean you are guaranteed a win. But I can't personally think of a situation where it hasn't. As a potential mark, the signs to look out for include learning three firms have been asked to propose, RFP language that deviates from a client's boilerplate language or style, a scope of work that is a little bit of a stretch, or an RFP from a large private client that has a stable of consultants.

How Do You Combat The Three Card Monte?

Unfortunately, that's a hard question to answer. Some will say that a good go/no go process will keep you safe from the Three Card Monte. While a solid go/no go process helps, it's not a cure-all. First of all, the procurement officer is not going to send you the RFP unless he or she feels that it will pass your go/no go decision process. They need to make it look like the procurement was competitive and fair. That is the whole point of the Three Card Monte. In addition, if you do not submit, you may run the risk of not being asked to propose on later RFPs. Another common answer would be not to propose unless you know you are going to win. If RFPs that you are certain to win fall on you like rain, that is certainly the way to go. But my unpopular opinion is there are always too many variables involved to consistently and accurately predict an open and fair procurement. The fact is, you are not the only one pre-selling work. To accurately predict a win, you have to have good evidence that the procurement is rigged in your favor. This means you are probably contributing or enabling the Three Card Monte.

Accepting the Three Card Monte seems to be the most common response. Be aware that it is out there and make a gut decision when you suspect you might be a mark. You'll find that most people do not object to being the winning firm in the Three Card Monte scenario.

THE GHOST WRITER

When a client asks an outside professional to write their request for proposal, this is called the Ghost Writer scenario. I knew an ex-procurement official from a large metropolitan airport authority that used this tactic quite frequently.

THE ROUND ROBIN

Sometimes corporate clients have a pre-qualified group of professionals they give assignments to in some order. In this case, your position in line may have greater impact on your chances than any other factor. This is called a Round Robin.

THE TWO PILES

I once knew an engineer who would receive many proposal submissions each time he released an RFP. Before reviewing the proposals, he would organize them in two piles: one of those firms he never heard of and one of the firms he considered "the players."

The first pile went into the trash. He picked the winner from the second pile.

Is this unfair? Yes. Did it allow him to spend less time looking at proposals and still make reasonably good decisions? Yes.

DIVIDE AND CONQUER

It is reasonable to assume that every member of a selection committee will review your proposal in its entirety. However, one ex-government official explained to me that sometimes your proposals will be broken apart and each section will be given to a different member of the committee. Each committee member will come back to the group with his or her assessment of the section he reviewed.

This is a way for the committee to evaluate each of the submitters' proposals without every member spending the time necessary to review all proposals. It is quite ingenious, if you ask me.

Chapter 5:

Reading And Asking Questions About The Request For Proposal (RFP)

Welcome To The World of Ambiguous Directions

Ah, the RFP. I've read thousands of them. Each RFP is a snowflake. Each RFP is special and unique in its own way. Whether it is called a request for letter of interest, a request for qualifications, a request for proposal, or a bid request; the RFP always asks at least two of these three things:

- What Can You Do For Me?
- Why Should I Hire You?
- How Much Is It Going to Cost?

READING THE RFP

Read every damn word in the RFP. That page you don't think is important, is. Read it.

RFPs Are Not Perfect

Personally, out of the thousands of RFPs that have passed before me, I have yet to see one perfect RFP.

The problems come when the RFP has confusing, illogical, contradictory, or ambiguous language.

You may just shrug your shoulders and say, "Well, I'll just give them what I think they are asking for." That is often the wrong approach. You have to understand that creating an RFP is no easy task. Especially, if you, as a procurement professional, have many other RFPs to write and get out on the street. What you often end up with are errors of copy and paste. Language may appear in the RFP that was originally intended for another RFP. It's a common and very human mistake.

That's why it's very important, as the proposal manager, to read these RFPs not as gospel, but as a document created for humans, by humans. Ask questions during the official question and answer period to clarify the intent of the RFP. Procurement officials and selection committees want to see proposals that allow them to make quick, informed, and correct decision.

Ask A Stupid Question, Get A Stupid Answer

I know your mommy said there was no such thing as a stupid question, but she lied. In the proposal business, there are stupid questions that can ruin your chances of success.

Here are some stupid questions that you don't want to ask:

• Any question that demonstrates your lack of knowledge regarding the type of work requested.

• Any question where the reasonable answer would place your firm out of the running.

- Any question where the reasonable answer would give your competitors an advantage over you.

- Any question that would insult or offend the client.

How To Ask Smart Questions

Most of the questions you come up with will be about unclear or ambiguous statements in the RFP. It will be to your advantage to ask the questions in a way which leads the client to provide the answer you want.

For example, you could pose a question so the answer will not only clarify the language in the proposal, but also make the case for hiring your firm stronger or uncover a weakness in your competitor's offerings.

Let's assume the RFP states "distance from client's office" will be an evaluation factor. If your major competitor is out of state, you may ask for clarification on how distance from the client's office will be weighted (especially if you know it had been weighted heavily in the past) or whether the price proposal should be all inclusive, including reimbursable expenses like travel costs.

Always ask yourself, how can I ask this question to get the answer I want?

Chapter 6:

Planning The Proposal And Executing Said Plan

Because Pulling an "All-Nighter" is Not the Optimal Proposal Strategy

"Execution is the chariot of genius." – William Blake

If you are staying at the office until all hours of the night to finally finish a proposal, there is one person to blame...you. I understand that so and so did not deliver on time and blah blah blah. But if you don't steer the proposal development, it will steer you.

Late night proposal sessions at the last minute are always due to poor planning that led to even poorer execution.

THE CARDINAL RULE OF PROPOSAL DEVELOPMENT

Never ever speak of when the proposal is due. When someone asks you when the proposal is due, respond that, "It needs to go out on _____." Always speak of when the proposal is "going out." This puts you in control of the timeline.

This practice is so second nature to me that you never hear the words, "It's due on," uttered from my lips.

KICK IT OFF

Every book on developing proposals will tell you to have a kick-off meeting. So, why do people sometimes fail to have kick-off meetings? In my experience, it is because the line between making a go/no go decision and starting work on the proposal is not always clear. Some go/no go decisions seem to almost go up to the wire, especially if getting the right mix of subconsultants is essential.

Therefore, making the decision to have a kick off meeting is sometimes a roll of the dice, but it is better to have it than not. If you have even remote confidence that you are going after the opportunity, schedule and conduct the kick off meeting.

"BASED ON YOUR CURRENT WORKLOAD..."

The best and most effective commitment you can get from someone is in front of a group of their peers and superiors. But you have to be respectful of them and their time. So the question to ask every member of the proposal team during the kickoff meeting is this:

> "Based on your current workload, can you
> commit to providing me with your completed
> pieces by this date?"

SCHEDULE FLOAT INTO THE PLAN

In the world of project scheduling, the term float refers to extra time in an activity. Activities with no float are typically on the critical path, which means if they are delayed, they will delay the project.

When scheduling the proposal effort, make sure that every major activity (especially those assigned to others) has float. If the VP's technical approach absolutely has to be delivered to you by Wednesday, for god sakes schedule it to be due on Monday!

Ample Time For Quality Control Is Non-Negotiable

As the proposal keeps getting pushed past deadlines, you have to steal time from later activities. Guess what activity goes on the chopping block? That's right, quality control.

Cutting quality control out of your proposal process is just about the stupidest thing you can do. Therefore, you have to make it clear, both with yourself and the team, that the time scheduled for quality control is written in stone. It can't be changed.

If quality control is scheduled for Monday and you are not done with your piece on Friday, you'll have to make accommodations that allow the team to start quality control first thing on Monday morning.

Don't Wait Until The Day It's Due To Check Up

I don't condone being a nag, but don't wait until a proposal team member's due date to check up on their progress. The reason is simple: if it slipped their mind, they'll bang it out today and it will most likely be crap.

Yeah, the famous architect Frank Loyd Wright designed his masterpiece Fallingwater overnight because the client demanded to see the drawings. First, Frank Loyd Wright doesn't work with you. Second, that masterpiece leaked and had structural issues.

Be Understanding

When working with the professional staff, above all else, be understanding of their other commitments. No architect, engineer, accountant, or lawyer ever anticipated a large amount of their time at work would be spent creating proposals. It is not what they dreamed of doing. It's just a part of the business that nobody realizes is paramount until it slaps them in the face.

The most bulletproof way to ensure your co-workers will do a great job working on proposals is to develop outstanding relationships with them that are built on trust and respect.

WAY MORE DETAIL THAN YOU THINK I NEED

Eventually, you will need information from the technical staff about what they did on past assignments. Whenever I solicit this type of information, I make sure to give this direction, "Give me way more detail than you think I need." Otherwise, you get information like this:

"I was responsible for the construction of the $13B World Trade Center Reconstruction Project."

That's great and all, but it doesn't tell me sh*t. What the hell does that even mean? What did this person physically do? Did they write the RFPs? Were they onsite with their boots in the muck or were they in an office with their feet up on the desk? Did they manage the schedule? Did they keep track of the costs and, if so, how? Did they directly manage subs? Were they the person who had to ask the Port Authority for more money? Did they give a rousing speech to the entire crew every morning and then lead them in a yoga routine?

"Give me way more detail than you think I need." You tell them this because they think the gist of what they did is enough. It is reasonable for them to think that because you haven't told them otherwise.

DUMMY BOOK

As we are making a proposal, we put together what's known as a dummy book. This is just a manilla folder that contains the latest and greatest pieces of the proposal. The completed sections get a sticky note on them.

Once we start a proposal, we are immediately making a dummy book. This way anyone can see exactly what the proposal looks like at any given time. I learned the dummy book technique while putting together large engineer/procure/construct proposals about a decade ago. It's a useful and timeless practice.

DON'T BE TIED TO LOGIC

This sounds like crazy advice. You and your proposal team will often want to write proposals that are logical. You want your proposals to "make sense." Right?

Not really. The truth about proposals is that mirroring the RFP submission requirements and rating criteria is always a better approach than writing something that is "logical."

Let me give you an example. Let's say you are picking up your sweetheart for a date. His/her father comes down to greet you and says, "Here is what I want to know: what time are you bringing my child home, where are you going, how are you going to get there, and how can I reach you?"

It might be logical to answer like this, "We'll be driving my car to Jimmy's birthday party at the roller rink, the phone number at the rink is 555-RINK, and we will be back here by 10pm."

But in the proposal world, that's a rookie mistake. You need to mirror the request exactly. The reason for this is two-fold. First, the initial review of your proposal is often done by someone who is not a decision maker (see chapter 4). Their job is to weed out the proposals that are "not responsive" or do not meet the proposal criteria set out. Second, proposals are usually judged by a committee using specific grading criteria. It's the proposal writer's job to make it as easy as possible to rate your proposal. Using logic often makes it harder, not easier for the reviewers to grade a proposal.

The real answer to dad's question is:

- I'll have him/her home by 10pm

- We are going to Jimmy's Birthday party at the roller rink.

- I will be driving us to the rink in my car.

- You can reach us by calling the rink at 555-RINK

People often find it hard to write like this because it seems illogical or wrong. But in the world of proposals, logic does not dictate. Your response should be dictated by the client's request and I can't ever remember reading an RFP that seemed logical.

A DAY TO TRAVEL

Proposals should not be sent overnight but should be sent by "overnight service." Simply because UPS and FedEx cannot be trusted when it comes to your proposals. They have no skin in the game. If your proposal gets there late, they will give you your money back. No big deal for them, huge deal for you. Give them an extra day and assume they will screw up. Assuming they screw up is a lot safer than assuming they won't and being wrong.

If your clients are local, just hand deliver your proposals or have someone from your office hand deliver them for you. But be careful about the kind of communication you can or cannot have with the client while delivering the proposal.

KNOW THY FEDEX LAUNCH POINT

Heaven forbid you miss the FedEx (or other overnight delivery service) truck, because then you'll need to take your package to the latest drop off point. Where I live, that's right outside the Philadelphia International Airport. You wouldn't know it was there unless you knew it was there. So, know where it is. Otherwise, you may find yourself taking a last-minute vacation to an exotic location (i.e. client headquarters).

FOR THE LOVE OF GOD, MAKE SURE IT GOT THERE

After you send the proposal, confirm it got there well before the deadline.

Chapter 7:

Forms And Other Long Lead Items

Oh Yeah, I Forgot To Do Those

Especially in government RFPs, you may find a bevy of forms to fill out, registrations and licenses to come up with, and insurance or other details to confirm. These are what I refer to as "long lead items." If these things are not done during the very early stages of proposal development, you may find yourself scrambling to apply for registrations you do not have, get forms from your insurance company, pay taxes to states you haven't worked in for a long time, find overhead approval letters from three years ago, and complete a litany of other things you don't want to be doing late in the game.

When it comes time to sit down and start producing this proposal, you need to complete the forms and other long lead items first. That means every form is filled out, signed, notarized, and sealed. It means that every possible registration, certificate, or proof of any kind is in your possession and is up to date. It also means that every attorney, VP, or accountant that needs to review items has. If you don't, you will kick yourself later.

You might view this as a small matter that you can take care of "later." Later is the worst time to do forms and other long lead items. Make them the first thing you do. That doesn't mean start them now and finish them later. It means get every one of these items done now.

Chapter 8:

Tools That Will Help You Write Proposals

Let Technology Do The Work For You

There are a few hardware and software tools that I use on a regular basis to help me in my proposal development endeavors. Let me explain some of these tools and how you can use them to make writing proposals easier.

LIVESCRIBE SMART PEN

The Livescribe Pulse Smart Pen does something quite magical. As I write down notes in a proposal strategy meeting, it records what is being said. When I go back to my notes, sometimes a few days later, I just click on a word I wrote and it plays back what was being said at the time. In addition, the pen has a tiny camera that sees and keeps track of what it writes. These notes can be synced to your computer so that you can retrieve the notes and associated audio at any time.

Let me give some examples of why this is useful. I'm often sitting with people talking about firm experience and strategies when developing proposals. Being able to quickly find what was said about a particular issue or how someone articulated a specific client benefit has been invaluable to me. It is also quite beneficial to have recordings of project managers talking about their completed projects. Few people have the note taking skill needed to record these conversations while remaining engaged.

For privacy reasons, I restrict my use of the smart pen to proposal and strategy related meetings. But even with that limited use, the

Livescribe Smart Pen gives me an ability that I consider to be a competitive advantage.

You can learn more about Livescribe at http://www.livescribe.com

TEXT EXPANSION SOFTWARE

As a proposal manager, you probably write quite a bit (at least you should). Writing takes time and sometimes you need to write a good deal within a short period of time. Imagine a world where you could write much faster. How much more productive would you be?

One of the challenges with proposal writing is the time it takes to tailor your message/content. There are generally two schools of thought in proposal writing: boilerplate and tailoring.

Boilerplaters use standard language for the majority of their writing. The benefit of this approach is speed. The downside is the ultimate work product can be less effective because it does not always speak to the client's specific situation and needs.

With tailoring, you write something that speaks directly to your client's specific situation. The problem is this type of writing takes significantly longer to produce. Many seasoned professionals claim that this approach takes too long. But tailoring is the best approach if you have the tools and ability to write significantly faster than the average bear.

When you tailor, you can't just cut and paste boilerplate paragraphs into your work product. But there are phrases, sentences, and even clusters of sentences you will type over and over and over again. Using a simple tool, you can automate this process, allowing you to write much faster.

Both Phrase Express (Windows) and Text Expander (Mac) are tools that allow you to type triggers into your document that will automatically generate text. Once you get familiar with using these tools, you will be astounded by how much quicker you can compose powerfully tailored proposals or other documents.

Let me give you a quick example of a text expansion trigger I use. This one happens to be for my email.

> Trigger: mycard

> Resulting Text: If you ever need anything at all, just shoot me an email. I'll be glad to help. I have attached my vcard (which contains my contact info).

You've probably written something similar about a million times. The difference is it takes me only two seconds to write it.

Both these programs work at the system level, so you will be able to use triggers in every piece of software you use.

This approach won't be as fast as the boilerplate approach. However, it will allow you to develop tailored documents significantly faster than you thought possible.

Advanced Text Expansion

What I have provided above is a simple explanation of how text expansion works, but the benefits expand much beyond that. For example, these programs also automatically correct commonly misspelled words as you type them. They can also serve as a personalized spell checker. For instance, I create text snippets for words that I commonly misspell or forget to capitalize.

They also can execute scripts (many are built in) and perform functions like adding today's date or working with text in your clipboard. They also can be scripted to fill out commonly used forms.

In addition, you can set up text snippets with what they call "fill ins." When you type in a trigger, a screen will pop up letting you fill in portions of the text snippet to make it tailored to the client.

The use case for text expansion is almost endless for proposal managers. It is a technology that I rely on heavily.

Phrase Express comes in both free and paid versions (I've only used the free one). Text Expander is around $30. Using one of these tools will save you significant time, allowing you to get more things done.

You can learn more about PhraseExpress at http://www.phraseexpress.com/

You can learn more about TextExpander at http://www.smilesoftware.com/TextExpander/

DRAGON DICTATION SOFTWARE

While I have it installed on my system, I'm not completely sold on Dragon Dictation software (available for both PC and Mac).

The premise is simple. You speak into your computer and it types what you say. The catch is you have to say punctuations like "period" and commands like "new line." It is just like I imagine the 50s were when executives dictated letters to secretaries.

My major gripe with the software is its accuracy. Maybe it doesn't like the sweet sounds of my voice. However, other proposal managers swear by it. I hear a quality microphone headset improves accuracy.

This software ranges anywhere from $100 to $200.

You can learn more about Dragon Dictation Software (Naturally Speaking) at http://www.nuance.com/

Chapter 9:

Creating The Proposal Content

How The Sausage Is Made

> *"The skill of writing is to create a context in which*
> *other people can think." – Edwin Schlossberg*

One of the most important things you will do as a proposal manager is create proposal content. However, many people find creating content to be one of the most difficult aspects of their job. There are essentially two pieces to the creation of content:

- Writing (Updating, Revising, or Creating From Scratch)

- Designing

While you might consider each of these two areas as separate tasks requiring specific skills sets, the reality is that writing and designing are really two sides of the same coin. Both writing and designing are governed by established principles. People who understand these principles can apply a systematic approach to both.

Because my expertise is in writing, I'll provide you with the writing formula and give you some general advice related to design.

THE PURPOSE OF YOUR PROPOSAL'S CONTENT

The purpose of content in your proposal is threefold:

- To Persuade The Client To Hire Your Firm.

- To Get Past the Box Checker (See Chapter 4).

- To Leave The Client With a Warm and Fuzzy Feeling About Your Firm.

Whatever content appears in your proposal must move your proposal forward in one (if not all) of these three areas. That's why I'm not a big fan of boilerplate content. If you think your boilerplate will do more than get you past the "box checker," you're fooling yourself.

When plopping in or creating content, ask yourself whether it solves any of these three challenges. If it only solves one, can you revise it to solve two or three?

If the content doesn't solve any of these needs, delete it or revise it so it does.

THE CHALLENGE OF WRITING CONTENT

Because some find writing content difficult, it's often a major cause of procrastination among proposal managers of all experience levels. People often experience "writers block" or complain that they don't know what to say. This is because they approach each piece of content in its own unique way. Even though many of us took classes on writing in school, chances are those classes never taught you the formula for writing proposal content. By applying the formula, writing content will become as systematic as cranking widgets.

THE BASIC RULES OF WRITING PROPOSAL CONTENT

The majority of time spent on creating content is writing. Therefore, it is important to address writing first.

When writing your proposal content, you have to keep in mind that all communication, including writing, is persuasion. The content that you create will be delivered to a potential client or teaming partner. The goal of that content is to influence that person's decisions. So, it is important to understand a few things about the reader:

- He/she cares first and foremost about their own needs.

- He/she will want to spend as little time as possible reading or looking at your content.

With this in mind there are a few established rules of thumb when writing:

- Sell the benefit.

- Keep it as brief, but not briefer, than possible.

- Spoon feed the reader.

- Focus on the action.

Sell the Benefit

"Sell the Benefit" is a phrase that you may hear when talking about marketing. This means the reader needs to gain a clear understanding of what he or she would gain from making the choices you promote. Often, proposal managers fall into the trap of talking about how great their firm is and forgetting to identify how it impacts or intersects with the reader. Readers tend to hate this "fluff" and will most likely skim or skip it completely.

The "So What?" Test

How do you know if your writing, "sells the benefit?" The most effective measurement of benefit selling is the "so what?" test. Here is how it works. After you write something, go back and read it pretending you are the intended audience. Picture yourself as that grumpy old man who used to steal your baseball if it accidentally landed in his yard. After reading each paragraph, ask yourself "so what?"

Let's apply this test to some examples?

Example: Our firm has been in business for 50 years.

So What Test Result: Fail

Example: Using the lessons learned from 50 years of experience designing high-rise buildings, we will ensure your design is technically correct, constructible, and cost effective.

So What Test Result: Pass

Example: We started with only three people and now employ over 100 employees.

So What Test Result: Fail

Example: With 100 qualified employees, we have the in-house resources to meet your current expectations and satisfy any changing needs.

So What Test Result: Pass

Let's give some real-life examples of the test in action. Here are two redacted write ups found on the websites of large mechanical/ electrical/plumbing design firms. How do these examples fair against the "so what" test?

Example #1:

ABC Engineers is a leading consulting engineering firm providing technical leadership, experience in design and quality service across all market sectors worldwide. In addition to our core mechanical and electrical design services, we provide additional consulting services to better serve our clients.

Example #2:

Business challenges often have solutions in technology, facilities, and processes. We understand what drives your business. Moreover, we take a partner's interest in your success. It is our belief that partners give partners a competitive edge. Our clients depend on us to bring an outsider's perspective and analytical ability to help them plan, phase, and reach their goals. Our ability to engineer, construct, and operate facilities rounds out that objective.

If you said example #2 passes the test and example #1 fails the test, you are right. Can you see the difference between these two paragraphs? Can you see how one speaks to you and the other speaks at you. Example #1 is not bad writing. It just does not "sell the benefit." Therefore, it is not persuasive.

Keep it as Brief, But Not Briefer, than Possible

Many proposal managers are under the delusion that people enjoy reading their long winded proposals. They will write a flowery four-page cover letter and expect a potential client to read it. However, if I sent them a four-page marketing letter about my marketing supply business, most of them would not read it. This is why it is important to keep it brief, because no one wants to spend his or her time reading your drivel.

On the other hand, some proposal managers keep it too brief. Too brief is when you don't sufficiently cover the benefits or address the audience's requirements. People don't like to read content that is too long, but they are suspicious of content that it too short. It screams, "This firm isn't the best choice."

How to Keep it Brief

Especially with proposals, clients will often ask for a large amount of information. So, how do you satisfy their expectations without writing the next *War and Peace*? Here are some tools you can use to help you keep it brief.

- Bullet Lists

- Graphs and Charts

- Pictures

- Delete Needless Words

Bullet Lists

By using bullet lists, you can often take large paragraphs and break them down in a more readable fashion. Bullet lists are easier for readers to absorb and it's more likely that they will take the time to read a bullet list. You can often convey the same information, but in bullet list format. Furthermore, important points or summaries often benefit from the use of bullet lists.

Why use bullet lists?

- Easier for reader to absorb.

- Conveys same information with fewer words.

- Helps emphasize important points.

Charts and Graphs

Many firms use charts and graphs to help convey a complicated process, concept, or method that would otherwise take many words. It is always good practice to use charts and graphs, as much as possible, to present marketing information.

Pictures

Some say that a "picture is worth a thousand words." And for the most part, that is true. If you can convey an idea or demonstrate a fact with a picture, do it. Using pictures in the right way can give the reader a break and help keep their attention. Just make sure they are relevant.

Delete Needless Words

Re-read your writing and try to find sentences that can be shortened by removing useless words. Concise writing does not contain unnecessary words. Every word should be essential to the sentence. Every word should earn its place on the page. For example:

> Due to the fact that our firm has designed twenty similar structures, we are eminently more qualified to design your project. (20 Words)

This sentence can be shortened to...

> Because we designed twenty similar structures, we are the most qualified choice. (11 Words)

Spoon Feed the Reader

We live in a world where people want their information easily and quickly. Some proposal managers make the mistake of forcing a reader to figure things out for themselves. That's not a great idea. You don't want the reader to have to decipher your message. Writing proposal content is not like writing a novel. Proposal content needs to be direct and lead the reader to an obvious conclusion. Be sure to directly state the conclusion within your content.

Make it easy for the reader to follow your writing. Use subheads, follow formats exactly as clients have laid out, and above all don't "beat around the bush."

In addition, we have the disadvantage of knowledge. We just assume that everybody knows the good and bad things about our firm. That's a terrible assumption. Here is a better one to use. Assume the reader knows nothing. If you don't explicitly tell them, they don't know it. Don't talk down to the reader, but assume they are starting from a blank slate.

Focus on the Action

There has been a good deal written about the use of active voice in writing. I recommend that you write in the active voice. In the active voice, the subject of the sentence is performing the action. Sentences that are written in the passive voice read weak and sound less important.

Passive Voice: The MEP systems were designed by our firm.

Active Voice: Our firm designed the MEP systems.

To make proposal content read strong, it is important to focus on the action. By focusing on the action, we describe exactly what action occurred. Let's look at an example:

> Mark assisted Pamona County with inspection during the $365M reconstruction on Pamona Bridge, in Audibon, NJ.

While it's true that Mark was performing the inspection services for Pamona County, when you read this sentence, Mark seems like a secondary player in our story. But Mark is really our hero. Here is how this would read if we focus on the action:

> Mark inspected the general contractor's work during the $365M reconstruction of Pamona Bridge, in Audibon, NJ.

In this sentence, we learn exactly what Mark was doing. Mark inspected the general contractor's work. The sentence is now much stronger.

THE FORMULA FOR WRITING PROPOSAL CONTENT

Now that we understand some basic rules governing how we can write more effectively, let's look at the basic formula for writing proposal content. The formula is in essence a story. Stories have always been a very effective tool for persuasion. They have been used to covey messages and influence behaviors since before the written word.

The formula also relies upon the use of a series of "persuasion techniques" known as the weapons of influence. If you look carefully, you will see this same basic formula being applied to everything from television ads to local news stories. The formula is used so much because it is very effective at influencing people's decisions.

The formula is as follows:

- Set the Stage (Once Upon a Time)

- State the Challenge (Damsel in Distress)

- Explain the Solution (Hero Saves the Day)

- Describe the Result (Happily Ever After)

This basic formula can be used to write nearly every kind of proposal content. Let us detail each part of the formula.

Set the Stage

During the first part of the formula, we describe the setting of our story. The beginning of your content must give the reader a reason to read the rest. Usually, proposal content evokes the weapon of "social proof" during this portion. By doing this, you show that you are speaking about a client or situation that is so similar or familiar to the reader that they can relate. Our hope is after they read the content, the reader will see the proposed solution as a solution that is also appropriate for them.

State the Challenge

Every good story has a damsel in distress. When we talk about a damsel, this could be a man, woman, firm, city, agency, or even the reader. The only real criterion for a damsel in distress is that they have a problem or challenge that they can't seem to solve without some help. Again, we want to make sure that the reader can see themselves in our damsel in distress.

Explain the Solution

During this part of the formula, we describe the solution and give examples of the solution in action. In most proposal content, you or your firm will be the hero of our story. The solution is how you solved the problem and saved the damsel in distress. In the case of a new service offering, this might also take the form of telling how the problem could be solved in a new and better way.

Describe the Result

Everybody likes a happy ending. The conclusion of your content should state how solving the challenge results or resulted in a positive outcome.

Below, I've provided an example of how proposal content might use this formula.

PROJECT DESCRIPTION USING FORMULA

Set the Stage

Pilster Pharmaceuticals is a world leader in providing life-saving and life-extending therapies for patients with cancer. Respected as one of the worlds most productive and innovative research organizations...

State the Challenge

Pilster Pharmaceuticals was in need of a new 150,000 sq. ft. Process Research and Development Facility on their Chicago Campus. The scope of the new facility included three laboratory floors, which included BSL-4 BioSafety Laboratory (containment and hydrogenation) areas and a ground-level entry floor. The building's plan needed to accommodate a variety of specialized research support spaces, administrative offices, research staff offices, conference rooms and an auditorium.

Explain the Solution

XYZ Engineering was able to achieve key client success factors by utilizing our ability to understand and communicate Pilster Pharmaceuticals' culture to the entire design team and keep the project on schedule, saving an estimated $5,000,000 that could have resulted from change orders. Based on our experience with Pilster Pharmaceuticals's master specification guidelines, we requested a review of the original specifications of the project completed by the in-house design team before final approval. This action allowed us to uncover potential problems in the design ahead of time in various areas including the fuel hood elevations, electrical routing and the UPS equipment. This resulted in increased system reliability, substantial cost savings and an estimated savings of 1.5 months in design time.

Describe the Result

Designed and constructed within the initial $20M estimate, Pilster Pharmaceuticals's new state-of-the art facility helps the company continue its valued research into successful treatments for cancer patients.

VARIATIONS OF THE FORMULA

Sometimes the requirements of the client or the format of a document inhibits your ability to use the full formula. Resumes and forms sometimes fall into this category.

There are several different ways to approach team resumes, depending on the services you provide. Some firms use bullet lists or the project name followed by a brief description to illustrate previous experience on a resume. These resume formats are typically used by design firms that work with standard structures like schools, homes, and churches.

Government resumes forms, like the SF330, require you to format information in a very specific way. In these situations, you may need to use a truncated version of the formula that uses just the last two parts. For example:

> Lead Electrical Designer. Joe designed the electrical systems for the Bank of Canada's $2B data storage and processing center. The center achieved a reliability rating of 99.9999% uptime.

PROPOSAL DESIGN AND GRAPHICS

Does the look of a proposal affect a buyer's decision? Many people will tell you that it does, but they are pulling that statement out of their ass. They have no idea. To my knowledge, there have been no legitimate studies on whether the design of a proposal for a professional services contract affects the overall outcome (and I have searched).

Therefore, the reality is we have no idea whether design of a proposal affects the overall outcome in any way. My personal opinion is the purpose of a proposal's design is to make it easier to read and comprehend. There is no reason to believe an amazing proposal cover or the perfect color mix will improve your proposal's chances in any way.

Here is my advice: find a very good designer and buy a proposal template off them. Tell them the typography has to be optimized for easy reading. Before hiring the designer, have them explain to you exactly how they are going to do that. If they don't mention the words leading and line spacing; kerning and tracking; and fonts, do not hire them.

Looking pretty and being easy to read aren't exactly the same thing. Many in-house and outside designers make things look pretty with no consideration for making it easier to read.

Chapter 10:

Choosing The Right Past Experience

There's a Formula For That Too

One day the question came up in my office about whether we should give our staff guidance on the order projects should appear in proposal resumes and experience sections.

The ultimate answer was, "I hope not." We decided that to some respect, it's a gut decision.

But then I thought, maybe it's not. Maybe there is a formula to picking the order of projects. So I went through, in my head, the process I use to order projects.

Using an example for design (in the private sector) and an example of specialty services (owners representation in the public sector), I tested my formula on paper.

And as it turns out, you can use a formula to determine the order projects should appear in your experience section and resumes. While the formula below was developed for architecture, engineering, and construction firms, it could be applied to other professional services.

THE RELEVANCE FORMULA

This is really a formula for determining the relevance of experience. Your project might match each one of these criteria:

- Client: It's the same client.
- Service: You performed the same service.

- Market Sector: The client was in the same market sector. For example, transportation or pharmaceutical.

- Facility (if applicable): The project type is the same. For example, bridge or lab.

- Attributes: Special attributes, requirements, or situations are the same. For example, the project must be LEED silver or BSL-3.

- Location: The assignment or client is in the same location (city, county, state, region).

   We can build an appropriate order based on the projects which have the best mix of criteria matches.

HERE IT IS

This is the formula, in order from best to worst projects to use:

- Client, service, market sector, facility, attributes, location

- Client, service, market sector, facility, attributes

- Client, service, market sector, attributes

- Service, market sector, facility, attributes, location

- Service, market sector, facility, attributes

- Service, market sector, attributes

- Client, service, market sector, facility, location

- Client, service, market sector, facility

- Service, market sector, facility, location

- Service, market sector, facility

- Service, market sector

- Service, location

- Service

By applying this formula, you will have the right projects in the right order every time.

Chapter 11:

The 10 Second Resume

You Are But A Narrative In Someone's Mind

Resumes are arguably one of the, if not the, most important elements of any proposal. In fact, the only other sections I could consider as important are the executive summary/letter or approach.

Resumes present a challenge to us. We want to give enough relative information about our people to impress the evaluators. So we pile it on. Or maybe this person's experience really isn't spot on, so you pile on information you think we be deemed impressive enough to overcome their lack of experience.

Unfortunately, in both cases, you probably offer so much information that it's hard for the proposal evaluator to really see what this person is all about.

THE SOLUTION

The solution is the 10 second resume. What I'm talking about here is not a resume that only takes 10 seconds to create. Sorry for getting your hopes up. Instead, I'm talking about a resume that the evaluator can look at for 10 seconds and identify what this person's narrative is.

WHAT'S A NARRATIVE?

A person's narrative is simply how one might pigeonhole this person. For example, somebody's narrative might be the environmental lawyer that's the remediation expert. A different example might be the forensic accountant whose expertise is in auditing GMP construction contracts.

You need to be very specific when determining someone's narrative. What is the evaluator really going to say about this person? It is highly unlikely for an evaluator to look at a resume for 10 seconds, put it down, and think, "This guy is the best highway engineer that ever lived." More likely, the evaluator will think something much more specific like, "this guy is an ex-PennDOT project manager."

Remember, the people in your proposal are going to get pigeonholed. That's why you have to spoon feed each person's narrative to the evaluator.

WHY 10 SECONDS?

The idea behind this is simple. The proposal reviewer is probably not reading every word in this person's resume. Especially if you have included the resumes of a lot more people than will be needed to do the job. This is often done in professional services proposals ("we need to show these guys our tremendous depth!"). You'll be lucky if the proposal reviewer looks at each resume for 10 seconds. So, in that 10 seconds, the proposal evaluator needs to figure out what this person is all about. Like I said, they will make a judgment about the person anyway, why not feed it to them?

EVERY WORD MUST EARN ITS WAY ONTO THE PAGE

There is one key rule you need to follow when developing a 10 second resume: every single word needs to earn its way onto the page. I know you probably love to put in as much detail as you can about a person's qualifications. However, it's like the old saying goes: if a tree falls in the woods, does anybody hear it? Similarly, if nobody reads the words you put in the resume, are they even there? Do they make your proposal any better? They don't.

Now, we would all like to think that most people read all the words we spend a long time putting together and making "just perfect." But if you've ever hired somebody, you'll probably admit that you don't spend 20 minutes reading each person's resume. Those candidates are lucky if they get 20 seconds of your time. Hey, I realize you received a ton a resumes to review for that position. The same is true for those who review proposals. Just imagine how many resumes that person has to look at to evaluate proposals from 10, 20, or even 30 firms that have proposed on the contract. When you really think about it, it's an astounding number of resumes. And, as the evaluator, you would have to be crazy to spend the time to read every word on every resume.

So, every single word has to earn its way onto the page. There are three ways a word can earn its way onto the page:

REQUIRED INFORMATION

The first way is to be required by the RFP. For example, some RFPs require that you state how many years of experience a person has.

"John has 30 years of experience in heavy highway and bridge construction."

Explicitly state it. Don't make the evaluator do math. Heck, don't even make them think. Who likes to think?

REINFORCES THE NARRATIVE

Another way a word can earn its way onto the page is to fit into the very specific narrative that you are trying to craft for the person.

Let's say this person's narrative is, "She's the project manager who manages the commissioning of HVAC systems in pharmaceutical manufacturing plants." While it might be impressive that she wrote a book about the ethics of construction, it does not fit the narrative. Therefore, that little tidbit gets cut.

If it is not 100% germane to the narrative, cut it. This is going to be hard for you to do. You will not want to cut "good stuff" from someone's resume. But if you want to create a 10 second resume, you must.

For example, if the person's narrative is they are "a plumbing designer who works on hospital renovations," then the fact they also typically design HVAC systems for the same hospital renovations is not germane to the narrative. So, you'll have to strip that out of his/her project descriptions.

PREEMPT A CONCERN

The last way a word can earn its way onto the page is if it preemptively addresses a concern.

This one is a little tricky. First, you have to have a good understanding of the concerns an evaluator might have about the person. Second, you have to legitimately alleviate that concern. If you don't provide convincing evidence that the concern is unfounded, you may do more harm than good.

Let's say you work for a firm that has recently been in the news because of ethical violations. In that case, it may be wise to identify that your project manager wrote a book on ethics in the construction industry. How can a person who wrote a book about ethics be unethical?

TESTING THE 10 SECOND RESUME

It will be very hard for you to test these resumes. That's because you have the disadvantage of knowledge. You know too much about these people and you already have a narrative about them in your head.

The best way to test them is to take the names off and show them to someone who may not already have a narrative in their head about this person. Let them look at the resume for exactly 10 seconds. Take it away and ask them to describe this person.

If they recant the narrative you created, then you've got the 10 second resume down. If not, go back and refine the resume a bit more.

Chapter 12:

Dealing With Unreasonable Page Limits

Tell Us Everything Your Firm Has Ever

Done and Keep It Within Two Pages

RFPs are notorious for requiring a ton of information and then slapping you with unreasonable page limits. You are left wondering how to fit all this stuff within the page limit.

WHY DO THEY GIVE YOU PAGE LIMITS?

Proposal evaluators want to get enough information to make a decision without having to read a lot. With each proposal submitted, the proposal evaluator's work grows exponentially. Therefore, they put page restrictions on the proposal.

It makes perfect sense. However, there is one problem: humans develop RFPs/proposals and we are flawed creatures.

WHERE IS THE PAGE LIMIT CALCULATION?

I would like to believe that procurement officials have a program or formula that calculates the pages necessary to address their requirements. However, none of the procurement people I've spoken to knew of one.

So, page limits can only be originated from one place: pulled directly out of someone's butt.

Page Limits Are Not Page Minimums

There is an element of our society that struggles with "loss aversion." Loss aversion is the tendency to prefer avoiding losses over receiving potential gains.

Here is how loss aversion works. Let's say I offer you a coin flip.

Heads: I give you $200.

Tails: You give me $100

Would you take me up on it? Most people wouldn't. However, logically speaking, it makes sense to take me up on my offer. Unfortunately, because of loss aversion, the pain of losing $100 is greater than the pleasure you would feel winning $200.

Page limits are especially troublesome for people who struggle with loss aversion. They are given twenty pages. They don't want to lose any opportunity to tell the client how great their firm is, so they demand that the proposal fill up those 20 pages. You could probably put a clear, concise, and convincing proposal together in 15 pages. But in their mind, the internal pain they feel by losing five pages of opportunity is stronger than the gain of a clearer and more concise proposal that the client might actually read. As an ironic result, proposals that have page limits often suffer from being too long.

How To Deal With Page Limits

Follow a few simple rules when dealing with page limits.

Rule #1: Determine up front how many pages each required section is allotted.

When reviewing the RFP, make an assessment of how many pages each section will take to complete. Then go back and see if that total number is below the page limit. If not, rework the numbers figuring out which sections it makes most sense to cut from.

Rule #2: Communicate the page limits. Then communicate them again.

Make sure everybody is aware of and is later reminded of the page limits associated with the section they are working on.

Rule #3: Don't accept a document that is over the page limit.

You can't put 20 pounds of dirt in a 10 pound bag. There is only one thing that is dumber than giving a marketing manager a 20-page technical approach and just assuming they'll somehow magically fit it on 10 pages: a marketing manager who takes it upon themselves to turn a 20-page technical approach into a 10-page approach.

Even if you make great choices about what to cut, you have now set yourself up for the fall if the approach scores poorly. Don't accept a document that is over the page limit.

Rule #4: Don't mess with the margins or make the font unreadable.

Some people will try to game the system by eliminating as much of the margins as possible. Congratulations to you. You found a loop hole.

Here's the problem. Proposal evaluators are typically older. Often, they are older than 30. Do you know what people in their 30s discover? Like me, they discover that they need to wear glasses. Making the proposal easier for you to develop, but harder for the evaluator to review is a fool's move.

Don't futz with the margins. Proposal evaluators are not stupid. They know what you are doing. Would you hire someone who gave you a proposal that didn't consider your ability to review it?

Remember, readability is essential.

Chapter 13:

Editing The Proposal

It's Not Right Until It's Right

Believe it or not, the area where problems most likely occur during the proposal development process is editing.

Let me start with this statement: there is no such thing as a perfect proposal. Yes, I said that. You have never submitted a perfect proposal, nor will you ever. The perfect proposal just doesn't exist.

Think of it this way. The New York Times, with a full-time staff of editors, is not immune to errors. Philip B. Corbett writes a regular blog post on their website about all the mistakes that readers find in the publication. These problems include logic errors, grammar usage, and even spelling mistakes.

Even acclaimed biographer Walter Isaacson, who was once the managing editor of Time Magazine and the CEO of CNN, is not immune to errors. Even I caught several writing errors in his Steve Jobs biography.

Heck, despite the numerous times I proofread this very book and the published authors who each performed an independent review of it, I guarantee there are several errors still in here.

Why is catching our own errors so hard? Part of the problem is how our minds work. Let me give you an example.

Eevn touhgh these wrosd are srcmaelbd, you can raed tihs praagarph. The order of the ltteers in each word is not ipmrotnat. But the frsit and lsat ltteer msut be in the rhgit psotitoin. The ohter ltetres can be mxeid up and you can sitll raed it whtiuot porbelms. This is bceusae our mind antipciates the nxet word.

Think about how easy it is for your brain to anticipate the next word if you wrote it.

OK, So What Is Perfect Enough?

Now, as far as your boss is concerned, the proposals you are going to send out are perfect. However, there is a different version of perfect known as "perfect enough." While you will never catch 100% of the errors in a proposal, it is expected that you catch 99.9% of them. This means that you actively look for the mistakes in a proposal, correct everything you find, and avoid adding your own. This is what editing a proposal is all about, making the proposal as close to perfection as possible. There are mistakes in your proposals, so search them out.

There are a few practices you can implement that will get you much closer to perfection and at the very least help you avoid "stupid mistakes."

The Hot Potato

When developing a proposal with a group of people, inevitably you will be asked to incorporate everybody's comments into the proposal.

If multiple people are editing one section of the proposal at the same time, this is going to be problematic. If these people are working in a vacuum (meaning that they don't see the other person's edits/ suggestions), it is going to be very hard for you to determine which edits should get incorporated and which should not.

In addition, one person's edits may affect another person's edits. This can cause the overall proposal to become inconsistent and, in some cases, just plain wrong.

The solution is to let people who are editing or commenting on the proposal know that each section is a "hot potato." When Joe is editing the approach, Suzy has to wait until he's done (and his edits are incorporated) before she touches it. This is part of the reason it is very important to plan for this time in your proposal schedule.

Editing Other People's Comments

Sometimes people will come to you with written comments on a printed draft of the proposal. It is your job to incorporate these edits into the proposal.

However, it is not in your best interest to blindly incorporate all of this person's comments into the proposal. As mentioned earlier, you have to play the part of the proposal's advocate. You need an understanding of the overall proposal and how each of these comments fits into the proposal.

In a perfect world, people would read an entire section and then go back to make edits or suggestions. Unfortunately, people make edits as they are reading it. The problem is they are looking at the trees and missing the forest. They are reading and editing one paragraph without knowing what is contained in the next paragraph. They may add a statement in the paragraph they are reading that is stated a few paragraphs further into the proposal. To make this edit will be adding redundancy into the proposal and possibly make it confusing.

You have to look at each comment and determine its merit. If you have a question about the validity of the edit, it is important that you ask. This might mean you have to walk up to your boss or the vice president and ask, "What's the intent of this edit?"

Four times out of five, it will either be a bad edit and need further clarification or rewriting. If not, you'll learn something new about the business or your firm. Either way, it's a "win - win" situation for both you and the proposal.

The Highlighter, A Proposal Editor's Best Friend

There is one tool no proposal manager should be without, the highlighter.

The best way to review and edit a proposal is on paper. Yes, I realize we are in the computer age. And while you ultimately will be making the edits on a computer screen, when you review a proposal it is best to look at it line by line on paper. You mark your edits with a pen or pencil and then make the edits on the computer. This may sound time consuming. That's because it is. But better and faster are not always the same things.

Like I said, you'll need a highlighter. Either grab one from the supply closet or use $2 out of your own pocket to buy one.

Once you are convinced that the edit should be made, here is the highlighting process:

1. Review the edit on the paper.

2. Make the edit on the screen.

3. Highlight the edit on the paper.

4. Review the edit you made on the screen to confirm it was done correctly.

5. "Rinse and repeat."

Using a highlighter in this fashion will help you never miss an edit and properly incorporate them into the proposal.

Track Changes: An Angel And A Devil

Track changes is a beautiful invention. But when two or more people go back and forth putting track changes on top of track changes, it's a damn nightmare. Let people know that it's ok to use track changes as long as only one set of changes appears in the document at a time.

Read Backwards Technique

A good way to catch mistakes in your proposal is to read each line starting from the last sentence on the last page and moving your way, sentence by sentence, towards the first line in the proposal. The idea here is that, if you assess each sentence individually, you are more likely to find mistakes.

FINAL FLIP THROUGH

After the proposal is complete and put together, we flip through every copy of the proposal one more time, page by page. The rule of thumb is that we need to find a mistake, and we always do. No matter how good you think your proposal is, it probably has at least one "boo boo" in it. That is because while we are working with the proposal we become "too close" to it and our eyes magically pass by mistakes (because of the mind's ability to anticipate). That's why it's most beneficial to have someone who was not involved in the proposal development perform the flip through.

Chapter 14:

What If The Proposal Doesn't Get There?

Five Proposal Nightmares You Can Beat!

As proposal managers, we are on the hook to make sure the client gets the proposals on time. We know it's always imperative to get the proposal in under the deadline, but what do you do when it doesn't get there?

"Why in the world would a proposal not get there?," you may ask. If you have been in the business long enough, you know that many factors can come into play and result in a problem with your proposal delivery. Most veterans of the proposal business have been in this situation at least once. If you have a solid understanding of this somewhat-taboo subject, you may be able to spin the situation in your favor or, better yet, not get into it in the first place.

Let's examine why the proposal might not make it to its destination.

PROBLEM: UPS/FEDEX/DELIVERY SERVICES

These services are great, right? They guarantee your package will get there on time or your money back. But what does that mean? Certainly, they will not give you $1M worth of lost fee if the package doesn't arrive. You'll be lucky if you get your $20 back. And you will spend more than $20 worth of your time trying to do that.

One critical flaw is that these services are run by humans, and "to err is human." Like any large organization, these services have people who hate their job, who are not above lying, and who probably just don't care. This could mean disaster for your world.

Solutions

- Always assume these services will make a mistake. If you give yourself two days for shipping (meaning "gasp" send the proposal a day early), and if you properly track the package, you have time to adjust for their mistakes.

- Always call the service to make sure that delivery is guaranteed by a certain time. You'll be surprised by the places they consider "too remote" to guarantee a delivery time. Also be aware that some procurement officers don't view your package as received until it is in their hands. So, you might want to familiarize yourself with the client's receiving and mailroom process.

- Don't be afraid to call. If there is a delay with your package, do not take the customer service person's word. Call the local distribution center responsible for delivering your package. The number can be found online. They have more power to resolve your issue anyway.

- If you hire a delivery person to hand deliver the package, make sure you have their cell phone number to call them and find out the status of your package delivery. If you are local, it may be a good idea to deliver it yourself and get some "face time" with the client.

- Never use hand-written labels. If someone can't read your writing or it's too light on their copy, they may just put a bogus address in there and say you gave the wrong address. I have had that happen to me.

- Always collect all the evidence. I was able to get a copy of that label and show the customer service rep that it clearly wasn't my handwriting.

- Always check for addendums to see if there is a change in delivery address.

PROBLEM: YOU ARE RELYING ON "LAST-MINUTE" PEOPLE

Sure, this is outlandish! Certainly, there are no professionals out there that will wait until the last minute to work on a proposal. And they certainly will not underestimate the time it takes to put everything else together and get it out the door. I don't know anybody like that and you probably don't either. But in case you one day meet a person like that:

Solutions

- Remember this is your responsibility. If there is anything you can do to work around them, do it. Don't wait for their piece to do everything else.

- Be proactive with help. If you feel confident enough to take a first stab at the technical approach, do it. You probably read a million of these and your best attempt might be equal to their version of "calling it in." It may be less intimidating for them if they only have to improve upon what you have already done. Just make sure your first draft doesn't end up in the final proposal.

- Be empathetic, often these people are "last minute" because they have too much on their plate. Think in terms of what you can do to help them.

- Never be late with your internal deadlines. You must lead the proposal process by example.

- Decide on a firm deadline for their section and then move that deadline back a day or two.

- Follow the cardinal rule: talk in terms of when the proposal is "going out" not when it is "due."

- Never lie about deadlines, but refer to the last two pieces of advice.

PROBLEM: E-MAIL/FAX

"E-mail me the proposal." This is music to our ears. No printing, no binding, and no delivery headaches, right? But this is the most common way for the client to not get the proposal. Folks, e-mail today is in a sorry state. Spam, viruses, and other baddies are flooding our e-mail systems. These cause computer networks to slow down, blacklist e-mails, filter out potential questionable e-mails, or try to communicate with your firm's server (hopefully they speak the same language). If any computers in the chain between you and your client are affected by these issues, it may slow down or stop your proposal from getting to its destination.

Solutions

- Use a read receipt, if you can: These things work about 55% of the time. Remember, a phone call confirmation is always better.

- Send early: Again, always assume there will be a problem.

- Call the client: Make sure it is several hours before the proposal deadline. Usually, if there is a problem they will let you know and you'll have time to resolve it.

- 0 is your friend: If you get the client's voicemail dial this number on your phone. You may be able to get to someone that knows whether your proposal was received.

PROBLEM: WEB-BASED PROCUREMENT PORTALS

Many large private clients rely on procurement portals to receive responses to RFPs. This trend is now growing in the public sector as well. While these systems are less prone to mishaps, they are not perfect.

Solutions

- Always carefully read the portal instructions: Usually clients will provide you with detailed instructions on how to use the site. Most of us have been surfing the web so long, that we don't feel that it is necessary to read the instructions. This is a mistake.

- Don't assume the submission is instantaneous: The client may give you until midnight to submit the proposal. That doesn't mean click the submit button at 11:59pm. Some of these systems convert your submission into an email or post the information to another section of the website and these may not be instantaneous. Often these services will allow you to review your submission before submitting it. Take this opportunity to perform a virtual "flip through" of your proposal, just like you would a hard copy.

- Make sure every electronic form is filled out. Before you click submit, many of these services may not be able to remind you that you forgot to enter your federal tax ID or Duns number.

- If the system does not send you an email or come up with a "thank you for submitting" screen, make sure you call the client to confirm the receipt of your submission.

PROBLEM: ALL ELSE FAILS

If all things fail and your proposal does not make it to the client on time what do you do?

Solutions

- Give the client a call as soon as you find out the proposal might not be there on time. Be nice, apologetic, and pleasant. Realize that you are still at fault, even though it's clearly not your fault. Explain the situation, but don't make it seem like you are giving excuses.

- Be empathetic to their situation. They gave you a deadline because someone else gave them a deadline.

- Make sure you have documented who you talked to, what happened, and when it's getting there.

- Ask if you can e-mail or fax the package until the original arrives.

- Review the RFP. Did they give you the wrong zip code or address? That has happened in the past. Nobody is perfect.

- Do not give them anything in writing that says your proposal did not get there in time, unless they specifically ask you for it. And even then, write it like it's an unfortunate happenstance. Evidence of the incident could spark a legitimate bid protest.

- Remember, you did all you could and you have a "leg to stand on." But that does not mean the client will accept your proposal. 99% of the time, if you follow these best practices, you should be able to correct or avoid the situation.

Chapter 15:

What If Your Proposal Is Rejected?

You Can Still Turn It Around.

Once your proposal gets rejected, you are pretty much screwed. The key phrase here is "pretty much." It is highly unlikely, but not always impossible, to get the client to accept your proposal. I can tell you from good authority that rejected proposals have gone on to win contracts. Here's how you should approach this situation.

When your proposal gets rejected, your first inclination will be to try to prove the client was wrong to do so. You're gonna want to prove that your interpretation of the RFP language was the right interpretation. I'm going to tell you this is the absolute worst approach. Trying to prove them wrong is going to be too hard to do. Let's face it, most likely, you screwed up. In addition, I hear that humans hate it when you tell them they're wrong.

You don' have to prove that your interpretation was right and their interpretation (or anyone else's) is wrong. You just have to convince them that the RFP language was ambiguous, meaning that it had more than one possible interpretation.

That's your pitch, and it needs to be a convincing one. Make sure you use the word ambiguous. Explain what you mean by that, if need be. The best way to do this is immediately upon notification and over the phone with the contracting officer/buyer.

This approach will work better for public procurements than private ones. Also, it will work better when multiple firms are to be awarded a contract.

Just remember, you're already out of the game. This is your "hail mary" pass to see if you can pull off a miracle win.

Chapter 16:

Pricing Proposals

What You Need To Know In Case You Are Ever Asked To Do It

Mike and Bobby are the most popular watermelon salesmen in the city. Each weekend they travel to the country and buy watermelons from the local farmers at 50 cents per melon. They load up their truck with watermelons and head back to the city. During the weekdays, they sit by city hall with a big sign that reads, "Watermelons: 2 for $1!!!" After a few months of this, the two boys wonder where all the profits went. Bobby says, "I know the solution. We need a bigger truck!"

This may seem like a silly story, but it is one that certified public accountants tell when they describe how many businesses today operate. As a proposal manager, you may become involved with providing pricing details to clients. Unfortunately, there are many types of services and pricing strategies in this business. It can sometimes get confusing.

While you may not be the expert on what your firm's services should cost, you should at least try to make sure that you are not selling your firm's watermelons for anything less than cost. Before you can do this, you need to understand the different pricing elements, structures and pitfalls.

ELEMENTS OF PRICING

The following are common elements of pricing that you should be familiar with:

Rates = What you charge the client for your time

Overhead = The cost of doing business

Audited Overhead = The costs of doing business which are reasonable for the client to pay (identified under the FAR Act (Part 31))

Fee = A percentage mark-up for profit

Escalation = A percentage mark-up for cost increases in later years

Multiplier = Pricing based on a multiple of a rate

Clarifications/Assumptions = The "knowns" and "unknowns" that you based your pricing on

Reimbursable Expenses = Expenses the are passed onto the client like printing, faxes, etc. Some firms take a 10% mark up on all reimbursable expenses. Depending on your client, travel may or may not be considered a reimbursable expense.

PRICING FORMATS

The pricing format you provide a client will most likely be based on the type of service and the preference of your client. Here are some of the pricing formats you might use.

Hourly Rates

A common pricing format within the consulting world is the hourly rate. There are different types of rates that you might want to understand.

Published Rates

Most firms have published rates. These are the rates you charge for each discipline or employee category. For example, you may charge

78

$80/hr for a CAD operator. That does not take into account how much each CAD operator makes. It's just a price that your firm agreed is reasonable for that discipline. Published rates take into account the cost of doing business and are usually developed with an eye towards realizing a profit.

Actual Rates

Actual rates are what people actually get paid. If Sue's gross pay is $2,000/week, she probably gets paid $50/hr. Therefore, $50/hr is her actual rate.

Blended Rate

Another kind of rate you may see is a blended rate. This is when you provide one rate for a variety of categories. If your project manager's rate is $100/hr and your designer's rate is $80/hr, you may end up using a blended rate of $90/hr. The idea is for the Designer to do most of the work, which will make the job more profitable.

Loaded Rate

Your loaded rate is the (Actual Rate + (Actual Rate X Overhead %) + Fee. State governments often ask for loaded rates. However, when providing loaded rates, it is important to have an understanding of overhead.

Overhead

Here is where things get a little tricky. Often you need to have an outside accounting firm audit your overhead rate based on what the Federal Government allows under its FAR Act. Most clients will pay all or a portion of your audited overhead costs. The calculation for overhead is usually (Direct Labor + Fringe Benefits) ÷ Allowable Costs = Overhead. Sometimes this is calculated as a percentage and sometimes as a multiplier.

Field Overhead

When you are proposing people to work in the field (the client's site), you will provide a field overhead. When your team works in the field, the client is not expected to pay for the worker's desk back in the office. This overhead number is usually lower than the home office overhead.

Home Office Overhead

Your home office overhead is the allowable costs related to working from your office. A sample overhead might be 160% of the actual salaries. This takes into account costs like rent, electricity, furniture, administrative salaries, un-billed time, etc. Some agencies will cap your overhead. They may decide that they are only paying 113%. That leaves you eating 47% of your audited overhead costs.

Real Overhead

As noted above, your overhead is often based on what the FAR Act will allow. Remember that lunch you took a client to? That is not allowable and ends up being categorized as a disallowable cost. Most marketing costs are disallowable. To get your real overhead you need to recalculate by adding in the disallowable costs. The way I look at it is Actual Rate + (Actual Rate x Real Overhead %) = Break Even Point. If your firm's Real Overhead is 185% and Sue's salary is $50/hr, then you should theoretically charge her at $142.50/hr to cover your costs.

Fees

Your fee is what you take on top of everything else to make a profit. For example, your standard fee might be 15%. You may even be taking an administrative fee of 10% on top of your subconsultant's cost estimate, even though they already have their own fee built into that price. Fees may be set by the client or your firm, depending on the situation.

Escalation

Most of us are hoping for a big raise this year. That's because we work hard and our firms base their businesses on the fiscal year. Professional services assignments are different. One assignment could last for several years. So, how do you account for raises and increased costs? The answer is escalation. This is a percentage increase you will add every year. This is another area that agencies like to cap. I've seen escalation capped as low as 0-2%.

PRICING STRATEGIES

Here are some of the ways you might put your price together (i.e. pricing strategies):

Cost Plus

You may be asked for Cost Plus pricing when working for government agencies. This means your cost (actual rate + overhead costs) + something. Here are some examples:

Cost Plus Award Fee/Cost Plus Fee

This is your typical "cost plus" work. Here you are taking a fee (like 10%) on your hours. For each hour you bill, you add 10% onto your cost. This is often known as a "loaded rate."

Cost Plus Fixed Fee

In a cost plus fixed fee environment, you are getting a fixed fee for the work. This amount doesn't deviate based on the number of hours you spend on the job. The fee is usually paid out in equal payments over the course of the contract period.

Cost Plus Incentive

This type of cost plus job provides for an incentive based fee to be determined at the end of the job, based on parameters such as target cost and target completion date.

Lump-Sum/Fixed Price

In fields such as building design, you may be asked for a lump-sum price. You talk to your project managers and write a proposal that says, "We will design your building for $500,000." But don't send that proposal just yet. There is something that your project managers may not have told you.

When you give a lump sum price, it is important to have a complete understanding of the scope of work you plan to accomplish. And it is even more important to know the scope of work you do not plan on accomplishing. For example, how many meetings do you plan on attending? Will you be performing construction administration/ construction observation once the project starts construction? Are you expected to participate in the commissioning of the systems? These are the questions you will answer in your Clarifications/Assumptions.

Clarifications/Assumptions

Most pricing is based on some assumptions. You may typically attend one meeting per month. But each client will expect different things from you. So it is important for you to write down the assumptions your price is based on. This is especially important in the area of Lump Sum/Fixed Price. If you don't do this, you may be giving the client more than you originally intended. Always try to clarify as much as possible with the client and incorporate that information into your scope of work. Any other assumptions you made need to be addressed in the proposal's Clarifications/Assumptions section. It is also a good idea to think about what other services you can provide the client. There may be an opportunity to offer some additional services that will add value to your client's objectives.

Multiplier

You may hear your boss say, "Price this at a 3.0 multiplier." That means three times the worker's actual rate. So if you pay Sue $50/hr, then you have to think of her time as $150/hr. Even if Sue's published rate is $110, to reach that 3.0 multiplier you will need to use $150 in your calculation.

Not-To-Exceed

Not-To-Exceed means just that. You are not going to charge the client more than the agreed-upon amount. If it costs you twice as much to deliver the agreed-upon scope, that is your problem.

Making A Profit

As stated earlier, your break even point is your Actual Rate + (Actual Rate x Real Overhead %). To get this Real Overhead, you will probably need to look at your audited overhead statement and calculate the number yourself. Once you have this number, you can compare what you are charging to your break even. However, keep in mind that the overhead is based on last year's numbers so that could change from year to year. It is still a good benchmark. Pricing out professional services can seem like a challenge. In the end, it's kind of like determining how much you are selling the watermelons for.

Always Triple Check The Numbers

Marketing folks hate dealing with numbers. I calculate numbers more than I would like. And like many proposal managers, I get nervous about making a mistake. One slight mistake in the numbers can cause a huge headache, and we all make mistakes.

Last year, one of our proposal managers took a stab at calculating numbers for a proposal. She asked me to double check her numbers, so I took out my calculator and started tapping. I said the numbers were spot on. But, were they?

The next morning she talked to one of our technical guys and ran a "what if" scenario on the numbers. After doing that, she had a gut feeling that the original numbers were wrong. Going with her gut, she triple checked the numbers. They were about $10,000 off.

The moral of the story is even when someone double checks your work, that doesn't mean they won't make the same mistake. It's rare, but it happens. And when it happens, the results could be bad.

It might be a good idea to triple check the numbers.

Chapter 17:

Pricing Professional Services

Why You Might Be Better At It Than Them

How could a marketer possibly estimate pricing for professional services? The "professionals" are the ones that know how much their work costs, right?

Let's put it this way. If designers and contractors developed estimates that were right on the money, the multi-million dollar a year firm I work at wouldn't be in business.

THE DARK FOREST

Marketers see pricing as a dark forest that they would rather not go into. Let me put you at ease. It is a dark forest that you would be wise to stay away from. It gets pretty risky and bleak in there and I can't promise you'll ever come out once you go in.

The up side is there is no up side. I have to imagine that more firms have screwed themselves by piss poor estimating than piss poor grammar. Estimating mistakes can be quite costly (no pun intended). So, you might as well stand yourself in front of a firing squad.

Here's the kicker, your involvement will probably mean more accurate estimates in your firm's proposals.

YOU MAY BE A MORE ACCURATE ESTIMATOR

I realize this sounds like the most insane statement ever made. I assure you it is quite sane. Allow me to explain.

Have you ever baked a cake? How long does it take you to bake a cake? I asked these questions to an experienced marketer.

She immediately said, "30 minutes."

Personally, I've never baked a cake in my life. I have no idea how long it takes. Here is how I would estimate how long it takes to bake a cake.

First, I would decide which cake I wanted to bake and get a recipe (Uncle Google comes in handy here). Once this recipe (i.e. project plan) is in my possession, I can estimate.

I have a list of ingredients. Do I even have these ingredients? If not, how much time is it going to take to get into my car, drive to the supermarket, find the things I need, get back to my house, and unload these items? Five minutes, right? No. We are probably talking more like 30 minutes.

Now I have the ingredients and the project plan right in front of me. How long is "step one" going to take me? Let's say I have to crack a few eggs into a bowl and beat them. I'm just going to throw the egg shells in the sink, so let's say I can get this done within a minute.

We are at 31 minutes.

What about the other tasks? I better pre-heat the oven: one minute. Throw flour into the bowl: one minute. Throw in butter and mix it in: two minutes. Measure and throw in some chocolate chips: one minute. Add ample amounts of corn syrup: three minutes. Sprinkle in some smiles and unicorn tears: one minute (again — new to this).

Now I can put it in the oven. I guess I have to butter up a cake mold and dump my cake mixture in: two minutes.

We're at 42 minutes. But I'm ready to bake this bad boy, which will take about 40 minutes.

We're at 82 minutes.

It is done baking. Now I can take it out of the oven and put icing on it.

Oh, it's hot so I better wait 20 minutes for it to cool. After that, I can cover this thing with pre-made icing in about five minutes (I'm sure homemade icing is better, but who has the time?).

The cake is done. But look around, there are egg shells, flour, and unicorn tears everywhere. So, I'll need to clean this up before my wife sees: 5 minutes.

- Broad-based gut estimate based on experience: 30 minutes.

- Step-by-step, detailed estimate based on a project plan: 112 minutes

I hope you see, clearly, that a step-by-step, detailed estimate based on a project plan is the way to go. Sadly, professionals rarely take this approach when developing an estimate. You, on the other hand, have to because you don't know what the hell you are doing. You actually have to think about it. That is why your estimate can be more accurate. You will be forced to think!

WHAT'S THE LUMP SUM PRICE TO DESIGN A UNIVERSITY ARTS CENTER IN CHEYENNE, WY?

I bet you're thinking, "I have no fricking clue." After you read this, you'll have a pretty good clue.

There are many different ways to price professional services. I've covered most, if not all, of them. When selling professional services, you are selling people's time. All pricing you do will be based on hours.

One of the toughest prices to put together is a lump sum number. So, let's put one together. We'll do it:

1. Step by step.

2. With data — remember, we have no clue.

Let's say you want to estimate your design fee for a 47,500 square foot university arts building in Cheyenne, WY. What you'll have to figure out is:

1. How much it costs to build a 47,500 square foot university arts building in Cheyenne, WY.

2. What the university is probably expecting to pay.

3. What you could probably do it for.

4. How low you are willing to go.

HOW MUCH IT COSTS TO BUILD A 47,500 SQUARE FOOT UNIVERSITY ARTS BUILDING IN CHEYENNE, WY

There are "rules of thumb" for just about everything in construction. Examples include, "measure twice, cut once" and "a university arts building costs $274.96 per square foot." Engineering News Record's Architect's Square Foot Cost Book is full of them.

Armed with this knowledge and some multiplication, we can deduce that a 47,500 square foot university arts building costs around $13,060,600 to build.

Then you have to take into account the location. Luckily, Engineering News Record's Architect's Square Foot Cost Book has another rule of thumb. 93% is the multiplier in Cheyenne, WY. This means multiply the cost by .93. A 47,500 square foot university arts building in Cheyenne, WY costs $12,146,358 to build.

What the University is Probably Expecting to Pay

Ready for more rules of thumb? Total design costs for university buildings are between 6-12%. Ironically, how much that percentage varies is based more on the University's endowment than the type of facility designed.

10% was the rule of thumb we used when I was with a design firm. So, we are talking $1,214,635 of total design fee (all disciplines). That's a good starting point and it may very well be what the university budgeted for. But it begs the question, what could we do it for?

What You Could Probably Do It For

If you were to estimate the time it would take you to run a marathon, what would be your measuring stick? You don't use other people as your measuring stick, you use your own running. You measure against your own past performance. That's exactly how you estimate what it will take your firm to do the work.

Guess who has that information right in their little project database. That's right, you. Guess who probably doesn't have that info at their fingertips — most professionals at your firm.

If not, the accounting department is your best friend. They have that information, probably even broken out by task.

Let's say last year you designed a 50,000 square foot university arts building ($13,473,040 total construction cost) for $1,100,564. It was a profitable job, your firm didn't get sued for design errors, and the client was happy. This means you designed it for 8.17%. Therefore, you probably shouldn't charge less than $992,357 for a 47,500sf building or you may risk the financial success of the job.

What Will It Take To Win This Job?

Between $992,357 and $1,214,635 gives you some wiggle room. That may sound like a big difference. But one time a firm I worked for lost the job by coming in a whopping $1M dollars above the winning firm's design fee.

In addition, there may be tough competition out there. You may really need to sharpen your pencil. People tell me we are in a recession. Maybe you can find a way to go even lower. But at $728,781 (a.k.a. 6%), you may be "buying the job."

TAKING IT STEP BY STEP

Now you know what the university probably budgeted for the design, both the high and low end of what you might charge, and a profitable design fee based on your past performance.

However, the devil is in the details. You can get an even clearer view by estimating each stage using the hours on the previous project and subbing in the pay rates of the people proposed on the new one. Make sure the travel hours and other details accurately reflect the location and situation of the new project.

Then ask your principal what the minimum multiplier for this project is. A good multiplier will range between 2.5 to 3.5. You take the hours and multiply them by the pay rates. You take this number and multiply it by the minimum multiplier provided by your principal. Adjust for the new square footage. Then add any reimbursable expenses you need to lump into the pricing. That's your bottom dollar number.

PHEW

I gave you this example because lump sum is the form of pricing that has the worst risk profile. You can really lose your shirt on lump sum pricing.

The things you have to remember about pricing are:

1. Sell the watermelons for more than you paid for them.

2. Measure against your own performance.

3. Take it step-by-step, creating a detailed estimate.

Unfortunately, these are the three things that firms often fail to do.

WARNING

This is a very introductory discussion of putting a price together. The further down the rabbit hole you go, the worse it gets. You may start by asking what makes up the multiplier. Then you find yourself debating FAR clauses on allowable overhead expenses. Next, you accidentally step into the world of labor variances. Then one day you wake up in a Mexican prison. Like I said, it is a dark forest that you would be wise to stay away from.

I jest. What I mean to say is that every minute you spend pricing services is a minute you aren't doing the things that make you a great marketer.

Chapter 18:

The Slippery Slope

The Nirvana of Proposal Writing

What would the perfect proposal do? The perfect proposal does one thing: it wins. The purpose of a proposal is to win contracts. Some may argue that the purpose of a proposal is to get you to the short list interview. That is true for some proposals, assuming your proposal does not factor into the final selection in any way once a shortlist has been made. In my experience, that is exactly how some clients, like the California Department of Transportation, operate. Other clients do factor your proposal's "score" into their final evaluation.

ADVANCED PROPOSAL WRITING

Let's go down the rabbit hole a little bit more. I don't know this for a fact, but I'm going to wager that the proposal that gets read is more likely to win.

There are advanced tactics that advertisers use to get you to read their content. If your writing is good enough, you can use some of these tactics to create a slippery slope: prose that it is tough to take your eyes off of.

But before I get into that, let's talk philosophy.

THE BASIC PHILOSOPHY OF ADVERTISING GREATS

Here is one concept that might be hard for some to grasp. You cannot create a desire for your product or service. Instead, you must focus the clients inherent desires to your service.

Eugene Swartz, one of the most successful copywriters in history, put it this way:

"Copy cannot create desire for a product. It can only take the hopes, dreams, fears and desires *that already exist* in the hearts of millions of people, *and focus those already-existing desires onto a particular product.* This is the copy writer's task: not to create this mass desire—but to channel and direct it."

What that means is the client doesn't really desire your awesomely great service. The client doesn't desire your amazing divorce legal representation, she wants that bastard to pay. She desires revenge. The client doesn't desire the added value of your 20 years of accounting experience. He wants to keep his money. His desire is to keep control and possession of that money (i.e. greed). The client doesn't desire your "full service" engineering services. She desires her office to stop being cold. Desire to get back at your stupid husband, keep all the money you earned, and be in a comfortable climate are inherently human. That's what Eugene Swartz is saying. These desires were already there. They weren't created by you.

Here is a story that illustrates this point.

I was working at a design firm. One day, the head of global engineering for a very large pharmaceutical company visited our office to talk about a new building they were planning. Of course, we had prepared. We were going to wow them with "six nines." That's an electrical system that has 99.9999% reliability (important for critical facilities). What we didn't prepare for was this guy brought conceptual drawings and he was looking to get into the details.

Unfortunately for us, this guy could care less about six nines. He wasn't going to have any mainframe computers in this building. But we kept pitching it. At one point, he got pissed and said, "If you mention six nines one more time, I'm taking these drawings and leaving." It was one of the most awkward moments I've ever experienced.

You can't sell someone something that will fulfill a need they don't have. The need already being present is essential.

They have this need and they want to know if and how you'll fulfill it. Hold on to this concept, because it is very important.

THE KNOWLEDGE GAP

Here is another concept. This one is a little more science and less philosophy. Use curiosity to get people to read.

What makes you curious? I bet you never really thought about that. George Loewenstein Ph.D., a researcher from Yale studied the underlying cause of curiosity and determined that it is caused by what is referred to as the "knowledge (information) gap." He wrote:

> "The information-gap perspective predicts that
> curiosity will arise spontaneously when
> situational factors alert an individual to the
> existence of an information gap in a particular
> domain."

Let me break that down for those of us that didn't attend Yale. Loewenstein's theory is when we discover there is something we don't know, we want to know it. That's why we gravitate to puzzles. That's why we pick up "Cosmo," Star Magazine, or Men's Health at the grocery store check out line. Those publications are great at selling us what we don't know (i.e. exploiting our curiosity).

In contrast, if there is no gap in our knowledge, we're not curious.

BUILDING THE SLIPPERY SLOPE

Here is the approach to building the slippery slope in a nutshell. The purpose of a heading is to get the person to read the first line. The purpose of the first line is to get the person to read the second line. The purpose of the second line is to get the person to read the third line. If you can get them to read the third line, you probably have them for a little bit, maybe a few paragraphs.

Make each paragraph lead into the next. After a few paragraphs, hit them with a subhead and start the process again.

Here's where the advertising philosophies come into play. You use your headings and subheadings to create a knowledge gap, which prompts the proposal evaluator to read the first line. In the body, you focus the client's preexisting desires to your service.

EXAMPLE

Let's take a boring bit of information that we're always asked for, but nobody wants to read: your firm history. Here is a real-world example of a well-written firm history, probably better than most.

> School Cafeteria Design Associates was incorporated on June 18, 1999. Jim Steel started the company in his garage after recovering from his first heart transplant. He founded the company based on one simple mission: "We exist to help those in need." This mission statement is the foundation of School Cafeteria Design Associates' existence, and the driving force of the company.

Here is how I might rewrite this in an attempt to create a slippery slope:

> **Why Would A Group Of Professionals Dedicate Their Lives to Designing School Cafeterias?**
>
> Jim Steel had just received a heart transplant. While laying in his hospital bed, he thought about his life, what it would amount to, and how he might use this second chance to make the world a better place. This contemplation led Jim to an unlikely epiphany.
>
> As an employee at a large design firm, Jim found his niche in the design of school cafeterias. He saw an importance to this work that maybe others didn't see. He saw an

opportunity to have a positive impact on an important aspect of a person's life. He believed he could design school cafeterias that would help children and adults develop healthy eating habits in a calm and safe environment.

But Could He Find Others Who Shared His Vision?

Jim resigned from his job at the big design firm and on June 18th, 1999 started School Cafeteria Design Associates in his garage, hoping to build a business. Over the next decade, he brought together a team of individuals who shared his vision and passion. Now with 12 offices, Jim and his team design cafeteria environments that children and adults, all over the world, love.

If you look at this passage, you'll be able to detect how I used the knowledge gap and played on my assumption that people building school cafeterias desire to create a healthy, calm, and safe environment for students and teachers.

You'll also notice a familiar format to this history:

- Set the Stage (Jim is sitting in his hospital bed after a heart attack.)

- State the Challenge (How can he use this second chance?)

- Explain the Solution (Starting a business designing school cafeterias that would help children and adults develop healthy eating habits in a calm and safe environment.)

- Describe the Result (Jim and his team design cafeteria environments that children and adults, all over the world, love.)

WHY TRYING TO CREATE THE SLIPPERY SLOPE IS EXTREMELY DANGEROUS

In my example, I assumed that, "People building school cafeterias desire to create a healthy, calm, and safe environment for students and teachers." The problem with assumptions is they can be way off. If you make an assumption about a client's inherent desires that proves to be wrong, you'll probably do irreparable damage to your proposal. Therefore, any attempt to create the slippery slope is extremely dangerous and should not be attempted by the novice writer or someone without insight into the client's true desires.

Conclusion

Just When You Were Starting To Get Into It

Proposal managers are forged through trial by fire. When we come out, we know all this "stuff" about developing and submitting proposals to clients. I think we take for granted the valuable knowledge that each of us has gained during this experience. We forget that other people don't know this stuff.

The particular knowledge we gain varies from person to person. I don't think anyone knows it all. For example, I had an experienced marketer, who has written extensively about proposals, review this book. He had never heard of a "dummy book" before. For the last 10+ years, I thought dummy books were common practice. In fact, I considered leaving discussion of them out of the book. But now the world, or whoever buys this book, knows about dummy books and can reap the benefits.

That's why it is so important to share the knowledge we have gained with others. Not only will you take away at least one valuable insight from this book, but my tombstone will get to read, "He brought dummy books to the masses!"

Never forget that what you do is important. Whether keeping people gainfully employed or winning a proposal that ultimately adds something amazing to our world, your work has purpose. The outcome of your work affects people's lives.

Go forth and propose!

Bonus Chapters

If you liked this book, there are FREE bonus chapters available at http://www.helpeverybodyeveryday.com/bonus-chapters.

Why not head over to the website to check them out right now?

Additional Reading

Like I said from the beginning, I didn't cover "how to" information about setting up a proposal process or putting a proposal together. There are many books that cover these topics. You can do a simple search on Amazon. I'm also told *Proposals: On Target, On Time*, by Dan Safford, is known to be a good one.

If you want to learn more about the obligations related to procurement in the government sector, I would suggest checking out *A Horse of a Difference Color: Marketing in the Public Sector* by Bernie Siben.

About the Author

Matt Handal is an experienced marketer, co-author of the *Marketing Handbook for the Design & Construction Professional,* contributing editor of the Society of Marketing Professional Services' *Marketer* publication, and moonlights as Twitter.com's @MattHandal. In his spare time, he hosts an open blog, HelpEverybodyEveryday.com, on Marketing in the A/E/C Industry and strives to help everybody everyday.

He can be reached at matt@helpeverybodyeveryday.com, will read every email, and field every question. So, please don't hesitate to reach out.

CPSIA information can be obtained at www.ICGtesting.com
Printed in the USA
LVOW101750230113

316973LV00034B/1682/P